Liv Torc is a spoken w  ers
the vast caverns and c   nd
planetary condition. A l   of
Exeter, host of the Rainb   ost
of the Hip Yak Poetry Sh   try
School and the spoken

In 2019 her climate change in-the-face-of-motherhood poem *The Human Emergency* went viral across the world. She also performed at Glastonbury Festival on the Poetry and Words stage and represented Somerset for the BBC's National Poetry Day celebrations. In 2020 she was chosen as one of four Siren Poets by Cape Farewell for a commission on climate change in the time of COVID. She also wrote and filmed a poem for the BBC's *Make a Difference* campaign.

Liv is the creator of the *Haiflu*, a UK wide poetry, photography and film project that uses crowdsourced haiku and images to tell the social history of life under lockdown. *Haiflu* has been featured in *The Times*, *The Sunday Times* and *Mslexia* magazine and is one of the only poetry initiatives ever aired on the BBC's Radio 4 *Today* programme.

Her first published book *Show Me Life* was released in 2015 by Burning Eye. She is also the proud author of *Banana Poems*, released in January 2021.

Contact

w: livtorc.co.uk

e: livtorc@yahoo.com

f: liv.torc

t: LivTorc

The Human Emergency

Liv Torc

Burning Eye

BurningEyeBooks
Never Knowingly
Mainstream

This edition published by Burning Eye Books 2021

www.burningeye.co.uk
@burningeyebooks

Burning Eye Books

15 West Hill, Portishead, BS20 6LG

ISBN 978-1-913958-14-5

Book cover designed by Liv Torc

The Human
Emergency

For the humans,
with love

What if we can't save the Earth?
What if the Earth can save us?

CONTENTS

PART 1 - THE EMERGENCY

PART 2 - THE HUMAN

THE HUMAN EMERGENCY

It's getting late,
almost half past eight
on a Tuesday,
and my nose is in my daughter's hair again,
a forest of sweet jasmine creepers,
my tears
      salty
        rain
          dripping
from her bright green leaves.
Why are you crying, Mummy?
she says,
flinging her spaghetti arms
around my neck,
squeezing.
I can't breathe.

I've just read something sad on the news,
I say,
prise her sticky fingers from my face,
shake her off,
look away
from the blue-grey trust
in her eyes,
now reflected in the tiny screen
in my hand,
where I can still see
David Attenborough's furrowed brow,
oil fields, coal mines, gas lines
burping clouds of unrelenting stupidity
into the earth's
       storm
        sodden
          hanky,
leaving tar-stained blood in the creases
between blue skies
and infinite space,

in this place
where oceans press plastic kisses
to the shore.

I try to smile,
try to say,
Nothing for you to worry about, my love.
But the lie is so big
it fattens my tongue,
so I bury my face in her warm skin
and breathe her life back in.

Back into my body,
into my bones,
back into my mother
and her mother before,
teachers, tailors and scullery maids,
        back,
            back,
                back,
until she's just a link in the chain,
not the end of the line,
not the last of our kind,
not her.

Then back even further,
to the beginning of everything,
when we crawled out of the oceans
and onto the shore,
sitting together
under the moon
with the mother of us all.

I know soon
she'll discover
the world we have left her.

They'll teach her in school:
the vacuum-packed oceans,
Slush Puppy icebergs,
species extinctions,
sun-boiled bats.
She'll see the big graph and prognosis,
and that will be that.

She'll run home through the May blossom,
sun on her face,
to ask me the truth
about our flat-lining race.

But I'm not a scientist,
I'm just a mum
and I'm more scared of that moment
than any other to come,
because the truth in the hands of despair
is as good as a gun,
and how can I give her the world,
just to take it away?

You see, I was five years old once,
clutching my Christingle orange
with the Jelly Tots
on cocktail sticks,
slid open the bathroom door
to see my dad at the sink.
Picking at the wood chip on the wall,
I said, *Dad, is there a God?*

He stopped brushing his teeth,
fog on his glasses
disguising his face,
the weight of my question,
the smell of citrus

hanging in the steam
between me and his answer.

One second... nothing.

Two seconds: he briefly considers,
but he is a man of truth and of science.
He rests his mug of tea on
A Brief History of Time
and watches *Discovery*
until half past nine
every night,
and he is always,
ALWAYS,
always
right.

Three seconds:
he lifts his toothbrush to his lips,
scratches his head.

No,

he says gently
and, with that tiny word,

God is dead.

I take my *No*
out into the hall,
into my life.

I carry it still to this day,
I have it right now,
but it's never served
me that well,
or him for that matter:

30 years all alone
in the home we all left
and never returned to,
my mum,
my brother
and me.
Even the cat
never came back.

He just sits every night
on his own,
with his *No*
and his science.

And I know if I were to ring him right now
and say, *Dad, is the human race over?*
Is there still hope?,
he would lift his pipe
to his toothless gums
and say, *Nope,*
and continue to smoke.

And that might be the truth,
but it's not a good answer,
because God may not exist,
but I know there is something:

powerful magic that weaves
in and out of our lives,
that pokes us and loves us
and wants us to evolve and survive.

So when she asks me that question
about the future of life on this Earth,
Dad, I've weighed up your truth
and I don't query the facts,
but I question its worth.

Isn't it better to say,

It's incredibly scary,
it's as bad as they say,
but you are alive
and you are a miracle?
And that has to mean something!

It's true
we might be standing
at the moment
when everything ends,
but your generation has the power
to save the whole world,
and I'm going to help you,
because I've got your back,
and I am a miracle, too.

And guess what?
There is something out there
more courageous
and potent than science,
and I believe it will help us
because I've touched it,
and felt it
and I've seen it

in you.

THE EMERGENCY

Saving the World

HARD TO SWALLOW

Last night
I ate some hate,
scrolling through
toxic rivers of debate.

It's sitting like a tabloid
in my throat,
feels like my love
for England
might be broke.

We are a jumbled union,
jacked on blame
and phobic, sceptic,
populist disdain,

bile now as much
a part of us
as rain.

STILL EVOLVING

At school we learned about evolution,
how sludge turned to ammonites,
then goldfish,
then scuttling crabs
that turned into primates,
then pirates,
then our mums and our dads,
that each generation clawed itself
from the womb of its past,
shrugging off history
like fast fashion that sags at the arse.

The wives' tales, the prophets,
the teachings and fables
taught us how to make medicines
and fix wonky tables,
how to stare down a wolf
with blood on its breath
and walk with grim peace
to the edge of our death.

We learned over eons and centuries
and difficult stages
how to manage crop cycles
through the long Iron Ages,
build ships out of trees
that were blown by the breeze
to incredible places
to exploit other races.

Our forbears' hammers
were stones, sticks, then spanners,
sprockets, pneumatics, robotics and rockets.
The fittest, the tallest, the brightest evolve,
while the sneaky fuck sociopaths
also do quite well, I am told.

We learned that our psyches
were complex and layered,
with bits underwater, entombed in deep ice,
but if you check through the footnotes,
we always were bastards, selfish,
self-righteous and pious,
but also brave, loving, funny
and unflinchingly nice,
and easily swayed by the right
and wrong kinds of advice.

Now it's 2021,
and some think we should be sentient beings:
the Dalai Lama, Space Jesuses,
with hover boots powered by poo,
our clothes made from human hair and bamboo.
The planet? An international space park,
an abundant, immense, intense Xanadu,
alive and in balance from ocean to shore,
pulsating with writhing,
wriggling and roars
and unintrusive organic
solar-powered family-run stores,
the perfect rainbow of people
of all seven genders
living in yurts, trees
and recycled polythene benders.

But we've fucked it, like toddlers
controlled by our superegos and ids,
burning the planet for a few squillion quid,
judging the past and each other
by the thrill of all that offends,
while out on the streets
the bigots are spray painting terror
on the doors of our friends.

Evolution sits sulking and scuffing its shoes;
it's spent too much time on its phone,
scrolling through clickbait hate news,
and it's looking at goldfish and humans
and trying to choose.

But if you scan back through history,
you realise none of it's shocking.
If the atmosphere's heating,
the bed must be rocking,
as we cut down our trees
and hang up our stockings.

It's just what happens when animals
are given the power of gods:
they greatly reduce the length of their odds.

At home, our four goldfish
are fighting like knives.
They've got too big for the tank,
and they won't all survive.

SOGGY TWAT

The breakdown man said
he had to pull a £50k Mercedes
out of the flood yesterday.
They just drive into it,
expecting it to part like the Red Sea,
Bluetooth glinting off the storm surge,
King Canute in cufflinks,
an entitled Icarus with waxed wing mirrors,
scoffing at the locusts in Africa,
the burning bush kangaroos in Australia,
as if nature was something
that happened to other people,
the UK now a polluted pond of bewilderment,
full of fat frogs who should have seen it coming.

I don't like to tell people bad news,
but his car was a write-off, he said.
Grim satisfaction and compassion
warred with his top lip.

He had just loaded my Clio
onto the back of his van.
My wipers scraped across the screen,
like petrified eyebrows.
They just gave up in the storm,
dragging their heels across my vision,
until everything was spots
and streams and frothing glass,

like the future was not worth seeing.

I sat up front and stared out the window.
He had jazz on low.
Water pooled excitedly along the roadside,
a billion expectant royalists
waiting for the Queen's tsunami,
a torrential ticker tape parade.

He wanted me to hook him up,
tow him back to the garage, he said,
but the water was over his bonnet,
and I'm only on minimum wage.
I'm not getting up to my knackers in that,
just because this guy's a...

He didn't say twat –
he was too professional –
but we both thought it.

I imagined the three-pointed star
on the nose of his car
winking like a 50p in a puddle,
an emblem which once stood for
world domination,
no better than the flag on the Titanic.
It's not going to be peaceful rebellion, is it?
We aren't going to fade into the end of days,
but sink into soggy despair.
A perpetual camping holiday from the 1980s,
forever trying to do a three-point turn
in a cul-de-sac with a trailer tent
in the rain.

Miserable, wet, eating cold tomato soup
around burning oil cans.
Relying on the kindness of neighbours
and the Green Flag man,
who earns less in a year
than Mr. Mercedes earns in a month.

It's the people on the ground in the waders
who are going to have to save us,
over and over and over again.

His engine must have flooded –
the electrics poached,
the brown water lapping
the cream leather interior,
reclaiming the carcass of consumerism.

I am still a God, he thought,
as he sat waist deep in cow diarrhoea.

KIDS' CLIMATE MARCH

The kids didn't go to school on Friday.
They all skived off in their thousands,
played Tory truant with Andrea Leadsom's inbox,
swaggered, like silly socialist sausages,
past Katie Hopkins' newsstand.

When we heard what they were doing,
we peered out of our office windows,
hands full of plastic packaging
and toxic toner cartridges.

The kids failed to listen to our elected representatives,
who warned of wasting precious time,
and the danger of disrupting schedules,
as they kept busy with their efficient,
swift and productive Brexit negotiations.

Instead, the kids persisted with their silly snowflake dreams,
went AWOL during English Lit and Art
to paint pithy, poignant, political placards,
bunked off Maths, Geography, Geology, Biology
to read educated articles on climate science,
biodiversity, extinction and statistics.

They ghosted Sociology, RE and languages
to meet together in socially conscious,
multi-faith, bilingual community groups,
missing out on Media Studies
to take part in panel discussion shows on the BBC
and launch powerful social media campaigns.

Then, by mid-afternoon, when they should have been
running in slow motion round the tennis court,
they could be seen marching miles through city streets,
with rosy cheeks and blazing eyes.

Simon Abbot, aged 15,
missed Chemistry and Human Reproduction

to hold Isla Finch's hand
outside the Bristol council offices.
When she told him she was scared
about all the forest fires and insects dying,
he drew a ladybird on her hand and kissed it.

Yes, we will all remember the day the kids went on strike,
while our leaders scoffed and sneered at them
from inside their Twitter feeds,
trying to squash their heads between their fingers,

all those ignorant, naïve,
selfish, planet-obsessed children,
playing hooky in History lessons
to save their own future.

F*@K YOU, DESPAIR

I don't know about you, but
the news is scaring me shitless:
the unstitching of ice,
the burning flesh and forests,
the clouds of smoke seen from space
and the world leaders in lion face ear muffs,
deciding what dinosaur toy they want to be
ten million years into a different universe.
Who wants to be the lumpy, spiky one
that ate its own planet from under itself?
What, all of you?

My husband has started smoking again,
and the news is making me so anxious.
I keep thinking,
Let him smoke –
the world is burning.
Even the celebrities are burning now.

Upstairs, my children are tickling each other,
laughing like gibbons.
Are there still gibbons?
The air is filled with flying toys,
hiccups and tantrums.

I'm so sorry for them –
it's a kind of motion sickness,
how parents feel when they think of their children,
the shrink-wrapped oceans,
the too-hot summers.
Guilt, terror and whitehot fury
that burns so cold it chokes our smiles
and gives every story book an Orwellian edge.

They will have to survive
inside the consequences of all of this,
and we know it.

The big unfreeze.
Buy less, travel less, Skype and sweat more,
try to like vegan cheese.
Pick through the ashes of their homes,
learn how to make fuel from their own poo.
They'll be good at that.

_____

It was a beautiful sunset tonight –
pink swirls and drop shadow clouds,
red leaves clinging onto defiant trees.

Deep breath, in and out.

It is still beautiful here.
Life still wins.

I bite my lip, taste blood,
open a bottle of wine,
arrange the magnetic letters on the fridge
to read, *Fuck you, despair.*

Tomorrow I will stop buying plastic bags.

MR. BUMBLE BEE

Pollinate me, Mr. Bumble Bee.
Shake my sexual cells from me –
I'm a WILD flower.

Don't tell me you're dying out –
I need to feel you buzz about.
Come, have your wicked way with me –
I'm a sweet, sweet pea.

Oh, short-haired *Bombus subterraneus*!
He never comes crawling up my sticky floor.
He's just a fading notch now,
since there ain't no hedgerows anymore.

But a lover doesn't need a home.
Bombus, why not be a rolling drone?
Love the stigma, fight the phone.

I need you, *Subterraneus* - stay, man.

Foxglove, iris, red clover, toad flax
and the delicate petals of the comfrey
still need your long, lingering loving,
Mr. Bombus Bumblebee.

Oh, how I still miss
Bombus ruderatus!
The largest of the garden bumbles,
he used to visit twice a week
for a disseminating tumble.

Now he hardly calls at all –
disease and infection fill his sneeze.
Since his habitats were stolen,
there's only sorrow on the summer breeze.

So, stay and fight your extinction,
find new hives and cure your ills,

for there's no fun being a WILD flower
if they take away
our five speed-buzzing thrills.

Besides, playing hard to get might be sexy,
but I don't find it funny,
so don't you dare give up on me,
my fuzzy little honey.

Pollinate me, Mr Bumble Bee,
shake my sexual cells from me.
I'm a WILD flower,

and you're more than flower fellatio:
you're the future of all that's edible and free,
the struggle for life on earth,
captured in the plight
of the humble bumble bee.

Bzzzzzzzzzzzzzzz!

SKY SPINNERS

You're a whizzer,
a woosher,
a sonic swoosher,
an air slicer,
a low-flying bird dicer,
an H2O ricer.

You're a ghostly, three-armed angel
standing at the gateway to the cloud kingdom.
You're waving, we're drowning.
You're a trio of eyebrows - all frowning.

You're a kinetic, kite-sifting light,
a robot soldier in the sustainability fight.
You're a thin man with a fat plan,
a small plug in a big dam.
You're a vibrating, vertical battering ram.

Armed, farmed and sometimes alarmed,
you're a three-headed snake, already charmed.
You're a flower power tower,
an eco wower,
weaving electricity streamers
for ideological dreamers.

You're a ghost ship made of air,
a beleaguered beacon of NIMBY despair,
a dangerous place for drying underwear.
You're proof we care.

You're propellers without planes,
the champions of change,
both comforting and strange,
moving with magnetic grace
across the Earth's frenetic face.

You're a semaphore warning, seen from space,

sent to save the human race,
like a match is sent to save the dark.

You're hope's art,

an apple put back in an empty apple cart,
a sail on the all new Noah's Ark,
a piece of Sellotape on a world
torn clean apart.

You stop my heart.
You start my heart.
You stop my heart.
You start my heart.

You're clock hands on a ticking planet.

SOMERSET

BBC Local Poets Commission for National Poetry Day 2019

From the road in Somerset,
a wilting willow man,
chased off the fields by warehouses,
pollarded by council funding cuts,
the bedraggled cousin of the Angel of the North,
staring down the M5,
holding out its guts.

Somerset.

People drive through fast.
We are a patchwork blur,
a consonant slur,
a place on the way to somewhere else
with better views or brasher lights.
We see it all
from the heights of our mystic tor
and ragwort depths of our flooded floor.

Pull back our hedgerows,
like an ancient prison grate,
follow us, like a tractor into traffic,
tip us, like a cow.
We are nuclear fission,
scrumpy-soused double vision,
a gypsy cart on the sweet track,
a steam train on its way back,
a festival of 400,000 eyes
looking upwards.

We are a Parrett full of writhing elvers,
a wild-eyed Exmoor foal,
a jilted witch
turned to stalagmite
in a Wookey Hole.

Centuries ago, we rode in on a tsunami,
danced to the drums
of the Minehead Hobby Horse,
the Girt Dog of Langport
snapping at our heels.

Now we are 400-village strong,
gold spun in apple blossom sun,
our smiles fermenting
on the tips of cheese-and-pickle
pirate tongues.

Somerset.

We keep our families and our elders,
but we cannot keep our young.
They leave the orchards
for the hipster beer
and strange idea
that something better can be found
in bigger cities,
other
towns,

while we weave and crusade,
unafraid to be homemade,
always on the levels.

DEVON, I MISS YOU

You know that I miss you, right?
The twisty-whisty, flick-of-the-wrist,
top-of-a-long-list,
lush, lamp-lit loveliness of you.

The debacle in your sparkle,
the honey-simmered whimsy in your words.
Your mossy sleeves, full of magic pennies,
silver does, leaping in the diamond flecks
of your vajazzle.

You're like that boyfriend
I never really deserved:
red rubble stubble,
hedgerow eyebrows,
tractor tears,
penis like Haytor.

You taught me that Beryl Cook
was a life drawer
and, if you love hard enough,
through the haze of green stuff,
everyone has an aura
like they've been skip diving
at Interflora.

You were my Totnes-London,
Exmouth-Paris, Exeter-Milan,
my late-teens-to-early-thirties lifespan,
and I miss your barefoot bravado,
spelt scones and avocado,
café dates with sexy fungi aficionados
(I like a man who knows his mushrooms),
Saturdays spent incommunicado,
trammelling your tracks,
losing my way
in the ley of your lines.

Once I made sticky monkey love
in the woods at Fernworthy,
convinced myself that I had invited
bad mischief from the Fae.
After that, I could never look
at a responsibly managed pine forest
in the same way.

Later that year,
I took my ash dieback spear
to the Two Sisters stone circle
to ask to be released
from the curse of my loneliness.

And I left you,
but you never left me.

It seems so long ago now
that I swam naked in your rivers,
sipped cherry brandy round sage fires,
ate coriander curry
and howled like a banshee
at your endless apricot sky.

You were a mirror to my wild weirdness,
and I miss you...

How accepted and special I felt
to live so long
inside your chocolate box
in woolly socks.

You know, you can smell the stars in Devon,
buy fudge in every village shop,
lick the moon like a lollipop.

TO ALL THE HATERS

Trip Trap
Trip Trap
Trip Trap

Who's that trip-trapping over my sense of entitlement
and howling canyon of low self-esteem?
said a pale, weak-chinned advertising executive,
who lives in his mother's basement,
with stained jeans, a poster of Donald Trump
and a sweaty hand gun,
lying on a pile of porn
and grey pants.

– It's me, a soggy white English woman
with an overly large jaw
and a basket full of optimistic opinions.
I'm off to the hills to make myself fatter,
so fat I'll finally be seen.

– Oh, no, you're not, Little Miss Feminazi!
First, I'm going to subject you to a litany of abuse,
threaten to rape you and kick you in the face with boots
crafted from the pelvis of the patriarchy.

– Oh, no, Mr. Troll, don't do that.
I'm too easy a target for your sharpened rotor blades of shame,
and, besides, no amount of consequence-free turd tossing
is ever going to Febreeze the stench out of your armpits.

Wait until my big sister comes along –
she's much tastier than me.

– Oh, OK, but don't go off and become successful and happy
and forget all about me.

– What's that? she said, through a mouthful of sweet, green grass.

Trip Trap
Trip Trap
Trip Trap

– *Who's that trip-trapping over my overwrought victim*
mentality, virtue signalling and inability to understand satire?
said a deliciously outraged friend of a Facebook friend,
with an obscure profile picture
of two dogs playing in a water sprinkler.

– *It's me - a lefty, middle-class, pescatarian poet*
trying to tentatively poke a knobbly stick
at the human condition.
I'm just off to meet Nigel Farage down the local pub
and place a Stephen Fry coaster under his pint.

– *Oh, no, you're not!* said the troll, feeling triggered.
I find the mere mention of knobbly sticks as abhorrent
as other people's perspectives.
After all, the Nazis probably had knobbly sticks.
Wait here, while I slander you a bit
through the Facebook feeds
and act like a one-man oppressed nation
trying to overthrow a brutal dictator.
I also have a friend who has three pages of notes
on your spelling and use of the semi-colon.

– *Oh, no, Mrs. Troll, don't do that.*
Instead, why don't you scan through
some old Christmas Number Ones
until you find some 40-year-old lyrics
to take completely out of context?

Or you can wait until my big sister comes along –
she's much tastier than me
and really loves it when you speak to her

IN CAPITAL LETTERS.

*– OK, but don't you dare try putting on anyone else's shoes
and going for a walk in them while I'm gone.*

*– What's that?, she said, letting her bare toes
skip playfully through the sweet, green grass
towards an abandoned pair of crocs.
Well, maybe not.*

Trip Trap
Trip Trap
Trip Trap

*– And who the fuckity fuck is that trip-trapping over my bridge
with their lack of hygiene, no basic human rights,
fixed abode, or legal country,
shoes like rotting banana skins on spider skeletons,
small children clinging to their heart like a cliff face?*

*– It's me, Mr Troll,
a human consequence of globalisation, climate change,
wars over oil, terrorism, brutal dictatorial regimes
and chaos created by foreign military interventions.
I'm just off to risk my life and the life of my children,
in the hope that I can reach the other side of this bridge,
sea, wall, line of armed police,
and the environmentally compromised grey, grey grass
beyond, and, hopefully, save my family from starvation.*

*Oh, and engender a right-wing uprising of prejudice and
hatred across Europe and the Western world, of course.*

Mustn't forget to do that.

– Oh, well, you'd better come through, then,

or, at least, wait here,
while I get Katie Hopkins
and the tear gas.

I CAST YOU OUT

Boris, I can't hear you!
I'm not listening anymore!
I don't care what horrors
or wonders are in store.
I'm sitting on the floor,
with my back against the door,
a garden centre leaflet,
some pizza vouchers
in my lap.
It's all more interesting than you.
That tiny money spider
making its eight-foot scuttle
across the battered leather of my shoe
is more awe-inspiring
and less urge-inducing
than anything you could ever do.

You are a snake charmer in Eton armour.
Your moptop, flop hair is meh –
there are a billion better blondes out there.
Your USP would wilt in the wind
next to the lion's mane magnificence
of German sea captain Pia Klemp
saving refugees from Libya's coast.
She is sexy, like Mad Max.
You are flaccid, like raising the threshold
of the wealthy's income tax.

I don't want you in my feeds.
My verges are wild flowers –
you are mown-down weeds.
Less Boris,
more trees.

I CAST YOU OUT

with every bit of my indifference to your charm.

44

I cast you out with the middle finger of my right arm.
I cast you out, like a plucky underling
doffing a sarcastic cap to a foppish squire.
I cast you out, like the constituents of Brecon and Radnorshire.

I cast you out with this carbon neutral scheme
to bring efficient cookers to Uganda.
I cast you out with this recycling bin
full of soggy Brexit propaganda.
I cast you out with every contradiction
and Boris bus you cannot hide.
I cast you out with the humanity which you have
fracked out of the nation's pride.

I CAST YOU OUT

with this kipper.
Don't let it slap you on the back.

Jair Bolsonaro, you are the stupidest man
who has ever tried to breathe.
Burning down the Amazon
is the Darwin Awards' greatest overachieve.
You may try to kill our air,
force the natural world into a zoo,
but take heed, Mr. Impotent Fire Starter –
snowflakes can put out infernos, too.

I CAST YOU OUT

with this burning ember in your money.
I cast you out with the screams of a hundred tigers,
a thousand monkeys,
a million trees.
Let them haunt your eyes
and howl like ghost trains through your dreams.

Farage, eye of newt,
face of frog,
milk of shake,
you are senseless static.
My interest has been piqued by your demise.
You are lager-soaked with lies.
I turn around in slow motion
and drink my banana smoothie without peeking.
Your mouth is moving,
but I cannot hear you speaking.

I cast you out into the Atlantic Ocean,
without a raft or EU-sanctioned regulations,
and with no protection from the United Nations.
I cast you out to a time when Royal Britannia ruled the waves,
and most 'normal blokes' were right-wing slaves
who died in gutters of pox pustule plague.

I CAST YOU OUT,

Hopkins, Patel, Raab, Mog, Morgan, Gove, Brewer.
The Nothing from the *NeverEnding Story*
is howling through your Twitter sewers.
No one cares, no one's looking,
no one knows what you are for.
I don't believe in you.
I don't believe in you.
Delete, delete, ignore, ignore.

Aaron Banks and Jeremy Clarkson,
I cast you out with Greta Thunberg's courage,
a power so potent it lures the demons to your eyes.
Rich, white men who take pot shots at heroic teenagers
should be properly exorcised.

I CAST YOU OUT.

Trump, you are Hitler's stagnant bile.
I cast you out with the twinkle of Michelle Obama's smile.
I cast you out with the song of the lark in trembling flight.
A plague on your golden tower!
A blast on your mirrored sight!
Remember, no one can see fake tan
in the endless nuclear night.

I cast you out
with all the power that's inside of me,
every mountain, every tree,
every witch hunt that rode the spine of my ancestry.

I cast you out with every acorn,
every veg box, every bee,
with the broken heart of every refugee,
with every human fighting for this planet and humanity,
with the hex of this X
in this box on this ballot,
with this little pencil on a piece of string.

I cast you out with this poem,
with this moment,
with this mantra
that you can sing.

I CAST YOU OUT!
I CAST YOU OUT!
I CAST YOU OUT!

May your teeth splinter with every lie.
Here's blood on your hands,
here's love for your heart,

here's salt in your eye.

SIRENS

I left climate change on the doorstep
when COVID came to tea,
washed my hands repeatedly,
scrubbed off endangered species,
gulped down the rising sea.

As the siren sun beat down
with record-breaking flare,
the Earth wrapped us in her riotous spring
and saved us from despair,

the future singing to its grandchildren,
swallows keening in the skies,
asking us to listen,
calling us to rise.

HOW TO MAKE A DIFFERENCE

BBC Local Poets Commission 2020

You get up.
You don't even have to get dressed –
just press your hand to your chest,
feel your heart and your breath.
That's a start,

and sometimes your heart
will want to be quiet
or sing every night to the stars,
transcending the roofs
and snugly parked cars,
so the double glazing of neighbours
seems less like steel bars.

You make a difference
by clearing the table,
sewing medical scrubs,
delivering the NHS food in takeaway tubs,
Zooming your parents,
shaving your head,
planting carrots and peonies
in your raised flower bed.

Every seed, every clap, every smile,
every time you step to the side
or walk single file,

you make a difference.

By sitting down with your kids and exploring their minds,
letting them chalk rainbows outside of the lines,

by chatting to neighbours you never spoke to before,
thanking the postman
standing six feet from your door,

by opening the window with the radio on,
letting news of community
swirl in the air with the trill of birdsong.

You make a difference
when you roll up your sleeves,
let yourself grieve,
do whatever it takes
to help yourself
and others to cope.

It's a lot about service,
but it's a lot more about hope.

YOU'RE *IT!*

Heart pounder,
coat swinger,
shoe scuffer,
giggle box,

you are hiding behind the school hut,
laughing so hard
the netball hoop you're leaning on
is shaking the fence.

There is a game afoot.
A knee twitches.
A body twists.
The air lingers,
as your arms fly.

Andrew runs at you
through the complicated warren of posts and bins,
chases you out into the open, like a rabbit.

He lunges,
clawing at your green book bag.
The Velcro tears, like a yawn.
Books scatter.
You stumble,
fall backwards into Noah,
a volcano of joy
erupting on the hopscotch.

The parents shuffle, grunt, unsure,
they wear their masks like bags
that have flown into their faces.

I steal tears away into my coat sleeves.
It's 8.55 am
and I don't want to embarrass
the queues.

But, in truth,
there is nothing more beautiful in this whole world,
no sunset, no siren,
no sweeping ocean vista,
no sweaty field of stars dancing,
than my five-year-old son,
hot cheeks, short breath,
playing tag with his friends
after twelve months of lockdowns.

Because that is what this last year took:
that moment when you race at someone
with your mouth open,
spit flying, face lifted, eyes laughing,
heart pumping, fingers splayed,
reaching across infinity,
through two metres of solid fear,
to grab fat fistfuls of puffy coats
and meet, skin to skin,
for a blissful second of connection,
before turning and launching on rocket shoes
to hide behind the scooter park.

COVID used tag.
It used touch,
it used laughter,
it used love,
and it turned them against us,

left my son hiding under the kitchen table,
alone and *It* for weeks at a time.

Pass it on.
Don't pass it on.
Pass it on.
Don't pass it on.

Childhood crusher,
hand scrubber,
joy snuffer,
face coffin.

You're *It*.
You're *It*.

You're *IT*.

THE HUMAN

Saving Yourself

CAKE ON FIRE

Happy birthday!
Happy birthday!
Happy birthday!

My cake is on fire.
Some of my bras are older
than members of this audience,
and nobody has said, *You don't look it!*
after asking my age
since I stuck my breast through the bars of a cot
and fell asleep with my face in the slats.

I seem to have arrived at the birthday
that nobody wants,
so close I can lick its jowls,
tickle its crow's feet.

There is a sign at the side of the road
saying, *Leave your nubile, dewy, rosy, silky bits in this box,*
next to Cinderella's glass slipper
and some girly currency that only works on bouncers.
Then pick up cholesterol, grey hair, short-term memory loss,
supplements, suppositories, unguents, creaking, clicking
and the inability to do the downward dog without farting.

The box is still a bit roomy,
so you can leave behind embarrassment,
the heartbreak you swore would haunt you forever,
and half the fucks you ever gave.

Then step through the peach-fuzzy curtain into 40.
You will know you have arrived
because you will start getting harassed
by life insurance calls during working hours,
and if you walk into a sports bar nobody will stare at your tits.

Yes, I, who once had a smile
that could charm my dad's friends
out of their salt and vinegar crisps,
have arrived at middle age.

Last week, I bought a 1000-piece jigsaw in W H Smith's
and I felt disappointed it wasn't 2,000 pieces.

I am clearly transitioning.
I should have been raging
through the final few weeks of my 30s,
hiking in tan shorts across alpine mountain ranges,
lounging on swanky beach furniture
wiggling my *on the cusp* cleavage
at tanned waiters with toe rings and man buns,
downing all the G&Ts
I can get my mother's hands on
before I become invisible.

Instead, I have broken out in ironic spots
from all the eye bag concealer
and spend my evenings googling photos
of beautiful women over 39
(mainly Helen Mirren and Tess Daly),
while fantasizing about owning a glue gun.

Yes, I have arrived at the interval between acts,
resting briefly in the crease
at the centrefold of my eyes,
an exotically named cocktail in my hand
that will devastate me in the morning.

But I can still touch my toes,
my hair is a low-maintenance lion's mane,
and I have never been so powerful.
So, fuck you, fear!
I wear my choices

like a catsuit of grooves and tears.
You can play jazz, Joni Mitchell
and Lady Gaga on my jaw,
and, after all these years of wondering,
I know that art is why I get up in the morning.
Art is what I'm really living for.

And I have learned that growing old
might not be fashionable,
but it's a privilege
not everyone gets,
a fucking privilege
to still be standing here
in front of you,
swearing,
frowning,
smiling,

ageing ungraciously

without fear.

Happy birthday!
Happy birthday!
Happy birthday

to me!

TIGER STRIPES

My body has got me to this moment.
Uneasy companions,
I have treated her less kindly
than a fairground goldfish in a bag,
an arranged marriage
full of distorted mirrors to disparage,
a hefty blown-glass pumpkin carriage
to pull around an acerbic queen.

My body is growing on me daily.
It bends, billows and farts,
kicks slices out of clouds.
It is steel and skin and crumpled carrier bags.
My body has Isambard Kingdom Brunel in its arches,
lightning scrawled across its belly,
but not the feathered fangs of womanhood,
a womb wild with writhing.
I didn't spit and claw and split
upwards from my pubic bone.

My stretch marks are not my tiger stripes,
but the silvery slug trails
of an overweight adolescence spent alone,
hiding in shabby bedrooms
from my father's divorce,
smuggling choc ices and Hobnobs inside my sleeves
as I crept heavily, dejectedly,
up the stairs.

They are the shadows of retreating shivers,
the visible vibrations of shame,
from a time when I was bullied daily for my body
and my name.

My body is the fat kid
I couldn't make eye contact with.

Now, in middle age,
I have ousted the standard Daily Mail,
playground, Twitter body hate
for a creaky kind of awe,
astounded by the power of my womb,
the molten mercury of my mind,
the valves and pistons of my thighs.

I wear my nerve endings like a mithril coat,
my senses a risk assessment, road map,
eyes like the Terminator,
full of statistics and streaming data.

My ballast is a boulder
between my children and the road,
my heart rosette a buttonhole, the perfect flower,
an oak blush figurehead nailed to my prow,
chewed, carved and sandblasted by black oceans
and soft-fingered sailors.
My arms are escape ropes that climb up to my lips,
my smile a skittish clown.

I am iron and muscle and effort.
I am milk and dust and lopsided love,
a crumpled balloon with a thousand kids' parties in its future.
My belly is a bean bag
I will always struggle to get out of.

No, my tiger stripes are not my stretch marks –
they are my eyeliner, my tattoos,
the miles I have trod to claw back my body from my past,
the ribbons and rosettes of my reclaimed pride,

because you can't keep eating your own dungeon,
just so you can hide.

BURY YOUR FEELINGS

What happens if the weather gets better,
but you don't feel better?
The periwinkle lid to infinity
is still covered in polythene,
and the daffodils, loud in your periphery,
only play Mozart on a dustbin lid?

What if the chill April slap
doesn't snap you out of it?
Nor the well-intentioned T-shirt slogans of your friends?
And when the swallows return,
superimposed against the fist of summer,
you can't look up –
your neck no longer bends that way?

But it's Tuesday, and, despite the grey,
you need some soya milk
and maybe a packet of biscuits,
so you carefully lock the front door,
tiptoe past the exploding cherry tree,
force your legs upwards
until you can't see your house,
or the Co-Op, or the dark river of sludge in your veins,

until everything below looks like a painting,
a blur, an insignificance.

Big is small, small is big,
as you sit down to dig
a hole with your hands,

somewhere to scream into,
or cough or sing,
until your secrets crawl out,
your voice cracks
across the shining backs
of escaping stag beetles.

Then cover your sacrifice with soil,
pack it in tight.

Let the worms have it.

And wait... and sit,
until you see a fox in the distance,
a red kite overhead,
or a face in the leaves,
a small sign that you are never really alone.

A reason to look up.

THE MOON AND ME

Occasionally I talk to the moon –
like, *properly* talk.
We have a late-night, moonlight
tête-à-tête,
tit-for-tat chit-chat,
her, I,
and the inkwell sky.

She brings the rocks,
I bring the gin,
the Earth sets the stage,
pumps in the oxygen.

And I don't ask about the small stuff,
because you don't go to the moon
with something you could google.

I always start with, *Hey, moon!*

Then she turns her full, lopsided,
pirate-treasure face on me and beams,
New York reflected in a puddle,
Excalibur in her teeth.

I say, *Remember me, moon?*
Remember me?
I mean, I'm not so young anymore,
or naked,
or standing in a field holding a spear.

In fact, don't look too closely:
I'm 40 now, I've got two kids,
I haven't done any proper exercise for a month,
and I'm wearing a tartan, fluffy dressing gown.

Can you even still see ME, moon,

now I'm not firm-flesh,
dewy-face, moon-maiden chaste?

She doesn't even blink:
I see you, girl! (The moon is American tonight).

She is even happy to see me.
I mean, she always sort of liked me,
but before she was kind of condescending.

She didn't find me endearing,
and I tried so hard to be endearing.
I was always asking her about boys,
and the nature of longing,
handing her my existential heartbreak
like a rare Mongolian artefact from 2000 BC,
as if she hadn't heard it more times
than the Rolling Stones have cranked out *Satisfaction*.

I once asked her if the man waiting for me in my tent
was crazy in a good way.
I mean, she would know.

She just stared, in smug, shimmering solitude,
twinkling stars on and off, like Morse code.
He's an S.O.S shipwreck in a bottle,
shot out of a circus cannon,
she blinked.

And he was...

But this time when I talk to her,
ask her about that thing I always ask her,
she isn't quite so bored,
she doesn't roll her eyes and sigh.
She has noted my sacrifice
in her big book of mother's tears.

She has counted the years
and knows the weight
of all the souls I juggle.
So, instead, she reaches out her silver arms
to hold me in a heart-to-moon cuddle.

Because the moon does not add
to a mother's struggle.

Are you still the same moon? I wonder.
Because you seem different.
Once you were like Judi Dench,
now you are more like Felicity Kendal.

Are you the same moon
who told me to hold my nerve,
promised me things were changing,
that love was coming?

Yes, said the moon,
unphased.
Exactly the same.

I pull my dressing gown around me in the chill,
and I hear a child crying upstairs.

She looks at me proudly, sadly, brightly.

I don't speak, or howl,
or make excuses
and I am already halfway up the stairs
when she whispers to my back,

Lovely one,
don't you know
it's you who is different now?

STICKY

You know how you can look
at your kids sometimes
and wonder where they came from?
How you actually made something
so wilfully sticky?
Worry that they are spoilt or selfish,
destined to become makeup vloggers
or young Conservatives
with pictures of Dominic Cummings in their wallet?
But, despite that,
you still - mmmmm, yeah, squeeeee! - love them,
like Lyra loves Pan,
like the moon loves the sea,
like the Queen thinks about death?

Every day, my kids fall,
and I don't catch them,
then I catch them
when I should let them fall.
They scream and backchat
and show startling courage,
while I eat too many carbohydrates,
try to get through till bedtime,
stick my head in the fridge
just to breathe.

Every Monday, I get in my car
and drive away - and it's a relief.

Then I accelerate home each evening,
my arms flung wide and eager
before I've opened the door,
before I've even stepped onto the path.

SCHOOL SHIRT BLUES

I found myself blubbing
as I did up the buttons on his school shirt,
big, fat tears that come when your last kid,
the little stroppy one
who still screams your name in the night
and clings to you like a monkey
on their favourite banana tree,
smiles at you proudly over a starchy collar.

You look back into his ocean-acorn eyes,
air filling your lungs in a *whoosh,*
and you are falling through time,
a blur of nappies, car seats,
tantrums, 4am bedwetting,
washing, bleeding, breastfeeding,
endless needing.
It all piles up behind your lashes,
like storm surge,
water and detritus,
oxytocin and wee,
while the bigness of what is still to come,
all the things you can't control,
spirals in on you,
past and future colliding
in a tiny plastic button.

My mum said she had taken the stair gate
down in the conservatory.
End of an era.
– *They aren't babies anymore.*
– *Thank God,* I said.

Of course, I loved those years.
They have saved me,
taught me what it means to howl human,
what the body and spirit is capable of –
sacrifice, sleep deprivation,

egg mayonnaise sandwiches –
what love can make bearable.

I hated those years, too.
They have bulldozed everything,
monopolised all of my loving,
broken me, aged me,
pulled my demons to my lips,
pushed me to the edges of myself.

My cousin said,
The main difference between
parents and non-parents
is that the latter still believe
they are good people.

It's true.

And yet his skin is so soft,
his eyes sparkle like stars in a jam jar,
and his first pair of school shoes
make dinosaur prints in the rain.

THE DRAINING BOARD

Our marriage monster sits on the draining board,
a precarious twelve-eyed shining beast,
with forks for ears, enamel teeth,
and jug-handle ears made from Perspex.
It towers over its tiny wire rack,
a Jenga jungle of clattering complicity.

I am in awe.
You are so skilled at bending the laws of physics,
balancing a spoon,
a plastic plate,
the blades from the blender,
a wine glass on an eggcup,
a gravy jug on a sieve.

Knives leap up like spawning salmon,
flashing their fins.
I catch them in my tea towel tangle,
wrestle their writhing blades to the block.

A stainless steel balrog burps from the pinnacle,
its belly now empty of stew.
Underneath like an abused mule,
the cheese grater squats, ridged.

Two soup bowls cling to the edge,
like Sir Edmund Hillary and Tenzing Norgay
pretending to be chamber pots.

I gingerly slide out a teaspoon,
inch out a spatula.
The spice rack coughs,
the tower shudders.
I breathe out, in tiny breaths.

I continue,
slowly, methodically
deconstructing your slippery sculpture
in tinkling silence,

accept the unspoken words
framed in the mouth of the beast,
caught in the teeth of every mug, dish and ladle:

Fuck you.
Fuck you.
Fuck you.

DON'T SAY IT

Hey, young buck, firm jaw... brave heart,
keep your beautiful, earnest,
honest, blinding love to yourself.

If you're sitting at home
with your finger hovering over a heart,
if you're lying in bed, nose to nose,
breathing their sweat through the ache of your neck,
if you're both the same age,
at a similar stage,
on the same sort of page,
then feel free
to use words like *love*,
mind-blowing, *synchro*-effing-*nicity*
my destiny.

But don't say it to me.

It's like being slapped by a lie,
its naiveties curse and, what's worse,
it's a clammy handshake
full of *give*,
laced with *take*.

I cringe now – at all those times
I made that mistake,
when I was brave-heart,
fresh-face, breath-caught.

When love was all that I thought,
and I said those words
to a man, or to men,
because there were more than a few,
and I thought that I knew
the mechanics of love,
because mine was so fierce
and righteous and free.

They'd just forgotten their worth,
and they could find it in me.

I didn't see the bags under their eyes
from the bags in the hall
that they couldn't unsee,
all those stains of shared history
with the woman they loved,
who would never be me.

Hey, sweet girl,
with your roar and your words,
don't say, *I love you* too soon,
not to a man
with snail trails in his hair
who isn't a fool or a fiction,
because it makes you appear like a child,
a child he will want to protect
from the love that has died in his hands.

Don't say, *I love you* to him –
it sounds far too much like,
You are going to fail
all over again,

and it won't be you in their heart,
but her, her or him,
on their mind, on their breath,
in their head,
on their lips,
as their shoulders imperceptibly shift to a wall,
and you blink,
and they've slipped out the door.

And now, now I have maps on my hands
and scars on my belly,
toddler seats in the car,

people buried in numbers,
lost on my phone,
and 38 years of *I love yous*
singed into my bones.

So don't say, *I love you* to me.

Because the man who sleeps
inches away in my bed
once found it so easy to say,
then life and kids got in the way,
and now it's scarce ever said.

If you have never tumbled
in slow motion from grace,
felt affection shift in and out of distaste
and truth slide into small talk and blame,

you might have met love,
but you don't know
the drag and snark of its name.

Young buck, firm jaw, fresh face,
I can hear the catch of your breath in the dark,
and my car is just a few steps to go,
and I'm walking away,

so please don't stop me to say,

Hey... I love you.

Don't say it.

Talk about love to the rafters and rooftops
and orange-streaked sky.
Say, *I love the shark-eyed moon
and the inkwell stars.*

Say, *I love this world
and this shitty Somerset town.*
Say, *I love that your smile
looks like a candle flickering
over the face of a clown.*

Say *I LOVE ME,*

and *I really fucking fancy you.*

But don't say, *I love you,*

because when you say that to me,

all I hear

is his silence.

THE SECRET ROLLER SKATING CLUB

There is this special club I'm in –
I don't know if you've heard of it?
I mean, it is a pretty big secret.
He's in it *(point into the crowd)*,
but he's not allowed to say.
They're in it, but if you ask outright,
they'll just shake their heads and slouch away.
She's in it, too... *Yeah, you! (picks out someone)*
She thought only her sister knew,
but I know, too.

I know about Prince Harry and Kim Kardashian
and my mate, Barry.
And the man from British Gas
who wears the big fake blonde moustache,
Justin Bieber and his chow chow, Todd –
he's got the moves and so's his dog –
Old Mrs Shankle, who – Newsflash shocker! –
doesn't have a dodgy ankle,
and the lollipop lady from your school.
What's her name?
Mrs Lucy.
Yeah, she's so cool.

We meet on Gratin Street
at half-past nine,
by the broken light,
when the moon drops like a bad penny from the night
to leave the world black as ink and burning coal.
That's how we like it,
that's how we roll.

High ponytails and slicked back hair,
Vaseline on lips and brows,
fresh and streamlined from the tub –
the members of The Secret Roller Skating Club.

We don't wear wheelies,
we don't like blades,
we're retro, roller-skating renegades,
carving up the soggy verges
with our nocturnal Disco Derby urges.

Whooshing, grinding, flashing, dashing,
we fly, falconlike, down icy hills,
with pavement panther precision skills,
leap over crates and under bridges,
glide through smelly alleys
with our fingers on our noses,
trailing glow sticks through garden roses.

We are so fast, we never make a sound
(or, at least, we're gone before the curtains twitch
and people rush out in their flannel dressing gowns
to stand aghast, with bleary eyes.
Did they just see will.i.am's retreating bottom,
sweaty thighs?)

Usain Bolt provides the skates,
shipped in from Paris in fidget spinner crates,
dyed black as the universe,
with a hundred tiny, jewellike stars
that glitter in the light of passing cars.

The club provides the anonymity,
a break from trolls and Twitter tedium,
the chance to all hold hands and skate as equals
into a secret world of bright cat's eyes
and pavement slides,
where even kings and queens can hide.

No one ever catches us,
we never leave a trace –
just a sense of something happening at speed,

of missing out,
and things that can't be talked about,

a trail of dust evaporating
into a dismal dawn,
as if the club was never there,
and we were never born.

But if you're ever out with friends,
and you see two strangers share a wink,
all touching fingers, toothy grins,
elbow nudges, secret things,
a furtive wave, a shoulder squeeze,
an earlobe twitch, a nostril rub,

pay close attention –
they could be members of
The Secret Roller Skating Club.

Best to forget it, pretend it isn't real,
unless one day you get the nod
about a meeting after tea.

I might see you there,
but I promise you –

you won't see me.

PARTY TRICK

Are you wonderful?
Are you weird?
Can you make your hair look like a beard?
Raise your left eyebrow in a question
and your right like a suggestion?

Can you whistle? Can you bark?
Walk a tightrope in the dark?
Curl your tongue?
Twitch your nose?
Play the piano with your toes?

Lick your elbow?
Go on, try!
You need to lift your arm quite high.
No, it doesn't matter why –
just give it a go!
It's all part of the show.

Can you rub your belly and pat your head?
Rub your head and pat your belly?
Put your feet behind your ears,
even if they're really smelly?

Can you make a wig out of your hair?
Have you tried? Do you dare?
Flare your nostrils?
Click your toes?
Write your first name in the snow?
They'll be turning up in droves
to see you remove your pants
without taking off your clothes.

Can you give yourself a hug
and touch your palms behind your back?
Wiggle your ears, like Jeff Goldblum
or a twitchy pussy cat?

Bend your thumbs back
to your wrist?
Open your mouth,
insert your fist?

Tie your tongue into a knot?
Touch your nose? Taste your snot?
Roll it out? Stretch it up?
Give it everything you've got?
Overextend?
How far can you bend?

Will your fingers do the splits?
Can you make fart sounds in your pits?
These skills are the perfect party tricks
to win you friends
(although I wouldn't recommend
turning your eyelids inside out.
I mean, what is that all about?).
What if you sneeze?
Your eyeballs might pop out
and land on your knees!

I'm feeling quite queasy now.

We are so wonderful and weird,
we should share
all the things we do in secret
when we think nobody's there,
because none of us is ordinary –
our bodies are extraordinary,
our skills are evolutionary,
our potential's revolutionary,
and some of us are legendary.

Can you whistle? Can you bark?
Walk a tightrope in the dark?

Curl your tongue?
Twitch your nose?
Play the piano with your toes?

Lick your elbow?
Go on, try!
You need to lift your arm quite high.
No, it doesn't matter why –
just give it a go!
It's all part of the show.

Now, every person,
everybody,
stand up, if you can, and take a bow.
Get up, right now,
and take a big bow!
Yes, all you at the back!
How low can you go?
Can you touch your fingers
face, forehead to your toes?

Now, stretch up your hands,
like you're reaching for a shelf,
and...

tickle yourself
tickle yourself
tickle yourself

No?

That one only works if you're tickling somebody else.

WIVES V GROUPIES

I'm a band wife
(not an illegal wife –
the wife of a man in a band),
and I've written this poem in honour
of all wives of men in bands.

The BAND
have got a gig next weekend,
he said.
You don't have to get a babysitter.
You don't have to come.
It'll be boring.
In fact, I think you shouldn't come.
There are some things you don't need to see –
like me, testing the limits of my trouser creases,
as I thrust out soft-rock riffs
into the snug of the Three Swans on a Saturday night,
to the delight of all the tangerine temptresses
from Sylvia Sullivan's wedding party.

I mean, the way they look at me, love!
Like wasabi on raw fish,
eyelashes two black crows on a garden rake,
gyrating in a cloud of blackcurrant vape.

It's so very different from the way you look at me
when we slouch past each other in the morning,
compromise and toddler snot smeared down our tank tops,
smiles cracking like crème brûlée under a blow torch.

And why shouldn't our dilapidated egos
be allowed a little innocent pick-me-up?
I mean, that shit feels pretty good,
like staring out at the fields on a September afternoon
and seeing a buzzard.
Or being nineteen again, and fitting blue lights
to the underside of a Ford Escort

before you go on a date with a girl
who doesn't shave her armpits.

It restrings your nylons,
makes you twang brighter.
It's a buzz, it's the Grrr! that sparks us to sing,
and when it comes to the intimate health of our marriage,
it's actually a really good thing.
Love...

It puts the whole world back in front of us,
like a yellow brick road to everywhere,
rather than night after night
looking in the fridge of your face
and only noticing the Branston pickle.

So, light of my life,
give me my groupies, and I will give you the world.
Or at least I won't spend so much time crying in the shed.

And you know, wives, we should
swallow down that scaly green lizard of insecurity
and let them go with joy.

We should even pick them out
some slightly more flattering trousers,
and, even if we are at the time
cleaning vomit out of a screaming child's eyebrows
and simultaneously trying to cook the dinner with our foot,
we should still kiss, kiss, kiss them goodbye.

And when it gets to 8.30pm,
and our brains start imagining scenarios
involving a Kate Hudson lookalike and a leather armchair...
then, and only then, should we slap ourselves
hard in the face and call a babysitter.

For, women and wives,
the great V's behind the great I's,
brush the toast crumbs from your cheeks,
remove that old fish finger from your cleavage,
leap up on the kitchen table,
throw back your proud, beautiful head,
and laugh, like you're standing on the bonnet of a Mustang,
with a cure for global warming in your pants.

It's time to take to the streets,
the stages, the soft carpets,
studios, classrooms and lecterns,
the lights, camera, action, catwalk of life.

Let him have his pouting Patricias
and stand-at-the-front, swaying seductively Susans.

Because we want OUR OWN GROUPIES!
Let them be young and witty
and hung up on every brilliant thing we say!

I want quizzical,
slightly abashed literature students
with Harry Potter spectacles
and leatherbound iPads
who approach me after gigs
and recommend novels to me,
playing nervously with the hems of their polo shirts
while they talk feverishly about poets
I have never heard of.

I want brashly tattooed troubadours
in brown leather jackets
to buy me stupidly named cocktails,
while looking at me intently, without blinking.

Who doesn't need a little
confusingly insightful empathy
from an unemployed marine biologist
who hasn't quite worked out
what to do with his sideburns?

I want to say things, like,
Oh, wow, you're really sweet!
and, *Of course, I'll sign your biceps
with my silver Sharpie!*
and, *No, I'm afraid a kiss
is totally out of the question,
but I will accept a full body bind,
while you whisper thrilling compliments
into my exposed jugular.*

Haven't we fucking earned
a bit of Mick Jagger's swagger,
a soupçon of Jimmy Page's ego rage?
Don't we all want to feel
a tiny bit like the Beatles in 1967
when we walk through the easyJet tunnel
at Bristol Airport?

Oh, let them have their sassy Saturdays
and the temporary thrill of being more than just a husband,
a dad, or a lawnmower operator,
with a nose hair trimmer
and a secret soft porn stash in the glove box!

Just untwist your undergarments,
pop open the Rioja,
call a responsible childcare professional
and acquit the inner hypocrite,
because, when it comes to groupie equality,
it's far better to admit
that you both need a bit.

Then you can return to the family bed
in the wee small hours of Sunday morning
as superstars,
with pockets full of promises,
diamond-studded genitals
and eyes like supernovas.

DON'T BE A TWIT,
BE A JOYFUL CONDUIT

I worry about you,
in the cubicle with the overflowing in-tray,
never quite able to get the hole punch
to line up straight.

I think you need something in your life –
a little next level?
The white light from
Leonard Cohen's bumcrack maybe,
cut with apple blossom
and Beyoncé's knicker elastic,
served on a fire poi?

That kind of shizz?

Well, I have just the thing,
so take your childhood dreams
out of combustibles
and get plugged in
to everything.

Let's rendezvous where the road
and rainbow meet.
Pay me with your hands,
your limbs, your feet,
and an intensity of focus
akin to hocus-pocus.

Oh, and you need to trust me.
I am your element, your muse,
the fool in flight,
a bright green satellite.
I come from the place
where Ziggy Stardust struts,
and larks ascend,

where the Show Must Go On,
and IT MUST,
take that on trust.

I've got a tongue that weaves
the ebb and flow
of spirits at a puppet show.
I'll quirk a brow, snap a brace,
smile like Disney drew my face,
and you'll just know,

like a desk light knows a frantic moth,
Van Morrison knows the Mystic,
the madness of colour knows Van Gogh,
a side of beef knows Lady Gaga's vital statistics.

Just look for me
by looking up.
I'll be the one burning
like a petrol fire
in a coffee cup.

I am the magic hour,
the *Tower of Song*,
Cary Grant emerging from the mist,
a flower like a tiny fist
punching through the gravel,
a thought that burns,
a die that's cast,
a busker singing through his mask,

the future phoenix of your past,
an answer to the thing you asked.

I am the beauty YOU decide –
not eyes or skin or shape,
but what your hands and mind create.

The more you breathe me in,
the deeper I'll go.
The more you make out of my madness,
the more sweet sanity you'll know.

I am the awen, the source,
a hypo of creative force,
and something else,
starts with a 'P',
rhymes with submission, transition, magician...

Take it.
Take it.

My friend,
you should have taken it
a long time ago.

Be a mark maker,
a disturber of the clean surface,
a gardener of hope,
an old soul kissed by gloss vermillion,
the 99th red balloon,
a haiku in a million.

So now I'm giving YOU the microphone,
hitching up your tights,
putting one hand on your shoulder
and the other

on the lights.

DISSENTERS' GRAVEYARD

I took them up the road
and round the corner
to the Dissenters' Graveyard.
It was high-summer hot,
and bright orange butterflies
eddied and twinkled.

They were thinking about ice lollies,
Rockets and Rowntree's,
while I was talking about all the lives under the stones,
trying to make their first steps over cold bones,
their first fingers on paper poppies,
their first touch of the names
carved into that yellow moss granite...
something soft and deep,
like skimming a stone across a pond
and counting the ripples.

I wanted to engrave in their minds
the opposite of fear,
the simple idea of a life well lived,
a breathing out,
like the moment you draw the curtains
on a summer evening
and pad upstairs to bed.

And as they whooped and skipped
between the overgrown headstones,
trying to clamber onto the green glass shingle,
I did that awful, stomach-churning
propriety-versus-poetry thing:

Don't tread on the graves.
It's not polite. It's not right.
It's disrespectful to the dead.
But also, at the same time,
don't be afraid to tread on the graves,

don't start your life afraid of stepping on death.

And as they wound their small bulldozer bodies
through this wisteria wonderland,
the people under the ground tugged
at my earlobes with grasshopper whispers,
poked at my shins with snapping twigs,

Don't you dare!
Don't you dare stop them dancing
on our forgotten faces!

We leave the graveyard and close the iron gate,
secure it with red baling twine.
A car whistles past as we cross the road,
its horn blaring,
too tight, too close for comfort,
and I feel sick inside.

My fear sidles onto the pavement
and follows us home.

The children laugh at a car
with skulls on the dashboard,
and the ghosts sleep on.

PEOPLE WHO ARE DYING
GET MORE PILLOWS
(How to survive a lengthy hospital stay)

Make the nurses laugh,
but refuse unnecessary enemas
that stretch your bowels like a rubber glove
in the hands of a children's entertainer.

Remember - a banana is not a good replacement
for a potassium drip,
even if you stick it in your cannula.

Request a commode twenty minutes before you need one,
and get to know which orderlies pull their masks down
when they think no one is looking.

Always ask people about themselves,
especially the cleaners,
as they have the best stories.

When a nurse says she is going on holiday to Northern Ireland
to tour the battle scenes from *Game of Thrones*,
don't ask her for a bed bath.

Other people's visitors will want to engage you in conversation,
particularly if you are wearing colourful pyjamas.
Don't be afraid to pull the curtains.

Having a shower and washing your hair
will make you feel as happy as Dolly Parton in a waterfall.
Giving out your conditioner is as close
as you'll ever get to Santa.

A bottle of lemon squash
is the most important thing on your side table –
it will make the full-time job
of consuming medication 78% easier.

Take the anti-sickness.
Don't underestimate the IV paracetamol,
but be suspicious of the Oramorph.

Giving blood will become a matter of pride and recrimination.
You will hear the words *sharp scratch* so many times it will
sound like a Buddhist chant.
You will bruise.
You will run out of viable veins.
Those who fail will call in bigger and scarier phlebotomists,
with tighter and shinier tourniquets.

You will not get a cookie.

Nothing happens at weekends,
but beware of Monday mornings:
they bring the phrases
– *We've managed to get you an emergency colonoscopy*
– *I'm afraid you ate five crisps,*
so you can't have a sedative.

Laxatives and drips are not good bedfellows:
prepare to drag the irate metal hat stand
out the door and down the hall
at least five times a night.

Sleep will be affected, interrupted and troubled.

Every morning a new consultant
will tell you something different
and every night their words will dance in your head,
in terrifying visions that give you nightmares.

Death might sit by your bed while you sleep
and hold you down by your arms,
and you will wake up sweating and paralysed.

Often you will push your buzzer and no one will come.

Be kind to the other patients.
Press your alarm as much for others
as you do for yourself.

Cry when you need to and don't apologise –
it gives other people permission,
and that's important.

If someone in the next bed is shouting or asking to die,
try to block them out with positive thoughts.
If you are shouting and asking to die,
take the Oramorph.

Try to remember if your eyes are open –
you can make that minute matter.
If your body is changed forever,
you can still find quality of life.

People who are dying get more pillows.
If you only have one,
you are probably going to be OK.

Suffering is awful, but try not to despair:
you are in hospital, where they keep the people
who can save you.

Keep breathing into everything.
Find the place inside where past and future has no meaning,
where climate change, COVID, your bank balance,
even your family seem far away.

Return home to yourself, with love.
Imagine you are just a leaf in the wind
and the human race is a layer of soil
on an archaeological dig.

You will learn that death can be seductive,
like becoming, returning, letting go,
locking the back door at the end of a very long day.

Living is the brave thing,

and you have to choose pretty quickly,
because they will want your bed.

SUE IN THE NEXT BED

On the gastro ward,
I was walking, hobbling
crawling back to life,
while you were gently letting go.

I felt the tiny candle
I'd been holding in my belly growing bigger,
to warm my feet and face
and the hospital windows,

my bedside a periodic table
of potassium drips,
smoking phosphate,
chewy calcium,
my body starved,
wrung out, bloodless.

At the other end of the bay,
your curtains were full
of soft Somerset voices,
talk of shower seats and palliative care.

Your daughter brought homemade lemon drizzle,
asked about the music for your funeral.
You loved the songs,
praised the cake, but never tasted it.

Nurses in grey dresses spoke softly
about holding on to the little moments
of hope in every day:
the colour of a banana,
your grandchildren's faces.

We fought to get you the perfect hot chocolate:
not too thick or sweet,
the smallest cup.

You hated the nights; we all did,
lying awake in the dark,
swimming in untethered hours.

When I passed your bed on my way to the loo,
full of cramps and clinging to my drip,
I would whisper the time to you.

– *Hey, Sue, it's 12.45am.*

– *Thanks, Lou.*

Two lives - one rising, one slipping,
shuffling softly in grace
through different exits.

You left the hospital smiling on a Tuesday afternoon
choosing *All Things Bright and Beautiful.*

After you went, I stared at the door
for a very long time.

THANKS, DAD

Thanks for the ulcerative colitis, Dad.
Every time I shit blood,
I'll think of you.

When I'm drugged off my head in a hospital bed,
chugging laxatives and morphine,
crying into my pillow – you, again.

I know you didn't mean to –
genetics picks its own teams.
I could have got your diabetes,
or kidney disease,
dyslexia,
total lack of self-worth.

I could have been a hoarder,
let myself slowly suffocate in my own filth,
slept on a divan base on the floor,
ignored the damp in the roof
until the ceiling fell in,
waited until every light bulb in the house burnt out,
so I could shuffle about in the dark
starving myself amidst cobwebs the size of a broom handle
and the tobacco-stained walls,
the toilet that requires acid to clean it,
and the gas leak you didn't seem to notice –
through the pipe smoke.

For the money in your account you claimed never to have,
the Christmas and birthday presents unopened in the rubble.

Thanks for the lectures about getting a proper job,
for telling the nurse it was *ridiculous*
when I told her I was a poet,
and because you have no teeth, only shards of bone,
she thought you said I was *talented*...

Thanks for this ugly, green flame in a bottle,
smouldering in my intestine,
the colour of burning plastic.

I want to chuck it through your broken window,
watch it set light to the piles of paper
you have kept for thirty years,
turn around on taser heels,
RIP open the sky and ooze away,
as your house explodes in my rear view
and my nightmares shatter, to reform
into your broken-down face.

Thanks for never letting anyone ever help you.

I will carry you forever in the dark places in my colon.

Thanks for leaving us with your hell, Dad.

Thanks for leaving us...

TELOGEN EFFLUVIUM

Haven't you got lovely hair?
the words of every old lady
since I was the age of four,
the midwife at my birth.
So thick, so much lovely hair!
glowered the hairdresser,
as she mentally stubbed out cigarettes
on my forehead.

My lovely hair fell out when I was 41
in haystack handfuls.
My Samson's mane of Rapunzel rope
that I thought would outlive me
was stronger than my spine.
That I inherited it down the generations,
a matriarchal lineage in helix,
my plait like a river python.

Blood over grit
Time over blood
Grit over time

Turns out it wasn't.
Turns out it didn't want to survive me,
but fling itself full body
out of my internal plane crash
in the hope of softening my landing.

For one hundred days it shed like a lawnmower,
got trapped in my armpits,
fur-balled my pants,
twisted round my toes,
added bondage to Barbie dolls,
broke the Dyson,
gathered in the washing machine
in giant hairy goblin testicles,
treated me like I was not in control.

My lovely hair.
Haven't you got it? Lovely hair!
That's what the nurses said,
and the woman who dusted
between the bars of my bed,
the orderlies that took me for X-rays:
Such beautiful, thick, lovely hair!

I had steroid skin,
pyjamas sticking to my back,
but my hair was beautiful.
They all said it.
Ratted and sweaty,
it felt like a rope around my neck.
I couldn't lift my arms to wash it.
I sat shaking in the corner of the wet room,
unable to lather the travel shampoo
or raise the shower head.
I watched the dirty water
run across my wrinkled breasts,
deflated stomach,
my eyes hollow in the thin mirror,
my hip bones sharp as my elbows.

My lovely hair watched me.
It worried itself in my shaking fingers,
and it made a choice.

It's your hair or your heart,
your locks or your lungs,
your curls or your colon.

12 weeks later,
I was crouching on the stairs,
trying to press it back into my skull.
You see, I thought I was getting better,

and all this hair in my hands
an afterthought, an insult.

Such lovely, selfless, stupid hair
sitting in a carrier bag by the back door!

What's left is a drippy, straggly weasel,
morning mullet, frizzy Worzel Gummidge vomit
that I'm so mad at!

I was 41 when my hair died for me.
– *Haven't you got lovely hair?*
Not anymore.
– *Yes, but haven't you got LOVELY hair?*
Yes, it's very brave, I suppose.
– *Isn't it lovely, though?*
It doesn't look it.
– *But it saved you!*
OK, yes, it's great when you put it like that.
– *It's lovely!*
Yes, OK, it's lovely.
Thanks, hair, you legend.

You are lovely,
after all…

But. Still.

Haven't you got a lovely colon?
said nobody ever.

THIS IS IT

I took my kid out to dinner tonight,
after school, to the café with a slide,
and her smile was so wide
because we never do stuff like that, she and I.

We ate hummus on toast,
and I scraped off the carrot
and unidentifiable seeds,
wiped her bum when she weed,
and she told me she loved me,
like she does every day,
then she went off to play with a boy
and some pink plastic toys,
and I played with my phone,
glancing up every minute
until it was time to go home.

Then, as we stepped out of the café,
the sky dropped like a sheet,
so we ran, hand in hand, up the street,
rain filling our mouths and blinding our eyes,
soaking our tights right through to our thighs,
squelching our shoes,
drenching our shirts.
It fell so hard that it hurt.

But she was so brave,
and she didn't complain,
as we swam to the car,
which I'd parked way too far,
in the roar of the rain.

Drying our eyes with her brother's clean pants,
which I keep in my bag
(not for this circumstance),
we smiled at each other
through our chattering teeth,

as I turned on the engine
and dialled up the heat,

and she whooped,
while I dripped,

and I said to my kid,

This is life.

This is IT.

THERE'S SOMETHING ABOUT MARY

I sat socially distanced at the end of your bed and said,
Let's get out of here, Mary.
Disconnect your fluids.
I'll put on my Asda disco pyjamas,
and you can push your own wheelchair, for once.

It's time to do a One Flew Over the Cuckoo's Nest
on the gastro ward.
We don't need Jack Nicholson off his meds,
or a seven-foot-tall Indian chief
to smash through the wall.
You can survive without solid food,
and I'm the only one who can open the door.

Then, it's just one shiny disinfected hall,
leading to just one more,
and we are sailing, cannulas trailing,
through the glass turnstile that hasn't moved since COVID,
past the huddled smokers clinging to their catheters,
outside, to where the sky meets the carpark,
the open fields kiss the skylark.

We can find that rowan tree by the bins,
let the drizzle swizzle our sweat-sour skin,
wrap our pin-cushion atrophied arms around the trunk,
pull down our masks and breathe her in.

Because we are not dead yet, are we?

Mary smiles at me.
She is 22 and has the rare genetic condition
Ehlers-Danlos syndrome.
She can't eat.
Her bones move about like barrels on a boat.
She has lost four stone in three months.
This morning, they dislocated her shoulders
putting her in the MRI machine.

At 7am we have not left the hospital,
as a disposable tsunami breaks over every ward –
aprons snap, bins clonk, visors steam,
masks stream out like ticker tape.

The Earth shudders.

Plastic reigns in here, and it makes everyone feel sicker.
There are no flowers allowed,
nothing living that can carry the virus,
no air conditioning.
The fruit cocktail comes out of a tin.
I can't even feel the rain
when I stick my fingers out the safety windows.

I feel so disconnected, it makes my stomach twist.

Mary asks if I'm alright.
It's Friday night,
and we are taking bets on her blood sugar.
How dangerously low is it?
How much liquid glucose
is she going to have to inject into her tonsils
to get them to leave her alone?

4.3 today, safe for a few hours.
Everyone is cheering.
Mary is doing air high fives with the orderlies.
Arnold is dancing in the aisles
with the blood pressure machine.

I love humans.

Sometimes, in all the fear and busyness,
I forget we are just Joni Mitchell lyrics,
Big Bang millionaire's shortbread,
not just supreme guilt gangsters

gasping for breath in a hospital bed,
but the atoms of everything,
as much a part of nature as the circling seagulls.

I look at Mary with the feeding tube,
laughing on the phone to her boyfriend,
sipping high-calorie energy drinks,
then vomiting them back up again,
plotting each tiny success,
sifting for diamonds in every coal sack setback.

It's like evolution is holding her up in front of me,
saying, *This is one of my finest humans.*
She may look broken to you,
but I made her,
and I'm as proud as a mother bear!

Mary looks at me, determined.
So what if they take your colon? she says.
You can still be happy.
You can still have a great life.

And she's right,

so I lay back on my sweaty sheets
that I've been sticking to all week
and think maybe Arnold
needs to take the Earth's vitals –

her oxygen levels are pretty low,
her UK temp is spiking at 32,
and you only have to read the news
or smell the air
to realise our world is pretty sick, too,

and maybe that's our fault,
but if COVID has taught us anything

it's that nature keeps on chucking out Marys,
dandelions and brimstone,
like it's Monday morning.

So neither of them gets my pity.

They are both just trying to find quality of life,

until they get to be stardust again.

THANKS & ACKNOWLEDGEMENTS

Thank you to the poets, the druids, my family, my employers, my proof reader, my publisher, the NHS and my colon. This book has come about because you and so many wonderful people have believed in me over the years and given me a platform to grow and mature as a writer, performer, human and artist.

So a huge thank you to my fellow poets and friends, with an extra poignant hat tip to Chris Redmond, Jonny Fluffypunk, Matt Harvey, Rozi Hilton, Francesca Beard, Chris White, Julie Mullen, Lucy English, Thommie Gillow, Shagufta K Iqbal, Pete Bearder, Crysse Morrison, Lydia Towsey, and Kate Fox.

Also to everyone who has encouraged, booked, employed and funded me as an artist, facilitator and producer, including Take Art, WOMAD, Poet in the City, Arts Council England, Cape Farewell, National Poetry Day, SPORK!, WORD!, NRTF, Living Knowledge Network at the British Library, Lincolnshire University, Artsreach, BBC Radio and TV, Burning Eye, Time to Change, MIND, Contains Art and Tongue Fu. Plus, all the others...

I have also been lucky enough to have met, befriended, loved, raged against, lost, danced and grieved with some very awesome and complicated humans, many of who have inspired the poems in this book or just helped me to be my best self. You include but are not limited to Adrian Rooke, Afric Crossan, JJ Middleway, Natalie Green, Damh the Bard, Mark Helyar, Sarah Peterkin, Gina Westbrook, Sarah Oakwood, Ruth Harvey, Natasha Kindred, Sundari Falconer, Sarah Winchester, Alice Walmesley, Boann Lambert, Amy Wragg, Hazel Barron, Julie Marter, Jon Powell, Jaime Shaw, Sue Howe, Elizabeth Cruse, Katy Tilley, Susannah Herbert and Mary Meilton.

Thank you to Melanie Branton for editing, proof reading and sorting out all my dodgy grammar. Also, Clive Birnie at Burning Eye for publishing my book on such a short turnaround and with such clarity and trust.

To my incredible husband, Richard Monks, marrying a pathologically honest performance poet takes much more courage than being one. You have my sympathy and respect.

To my mum, Mo Bennett, for a lifetime of support and laughter and all my extended family. To my children Wilf and Matilda, you will always be the very best part of my creative endeavours and my life. I love you more than poetry! Even though, you will argue, it doesn't often feel like it.

Oh, and thanks to the NHS for saving my life and my colon and to myself for being my very best friend in the dark and scary moments.

Finally, to the solid Earth beneath my feet, always the biggest person in the room and to the sun and moon, for rising above it.